Table of Conten

MW01269119

CHAPTER ONE: INTRODUCTION TO CANNING........3

HISTORICAL BACKGROUND..3
BENEFITS OF CANNING...4

CHAPTER TWO: TECHNIQUES AND RULES 6

TECHNIQUES FOR PRESERVING FOOD: 6
METHODS OF PACKING: 11

CHAPTER THREE: CANNING VEGETABLES...........17

PICKLES..18
QUICK PICKLES 21
GARLIC DILL PICKLES 24
JALAPENO RINGS...27
TOMATO SALSA..29
ONION JAM..31
CORN RELISH 33
CARROT AND CABBAGE JARS 35
CAULIFLOWER ZUCCHINI PRESERVE 37
PEPPER GARLIC JELLY 39
SWEET POTATOES 41
PICKLED BEETS 44
CANNED ASPARAGUS 46
PUMPKIN BUTTER 49
LIME JELLY...51
GREEN BEANS 53
RHUBARB 55
MIXED VEGETABLE JAR 57

CHAPTER FOUR: FRUIT CANNING 59

STRAWBERRY JAM 59
QUICK STRAWBERRY JAM...61
BLUEBERRY JAM 63
FIG JAM 65
APPLE BANANA BUTTER 68
APRICOT JAM 71
PEACH PRESERVE 73
APPLE BUTTER 76
PINA COLADA JELLY 78
HONEYED ORANGES...80
PLUMS 82
SPICED CHERRIES AND RASPBERRIES................................84

BANANA BUTTER 86

CHAPTER FIVE: MORE CANNING **88**

YOGURT AND BERRY PARFAIT 88
JAR CUPCAKES 90
MOROCCAN SALAD 92
THAI DIPPING SAUCE 94
CARAMEL CORN WITH NUTS 96
BARBECUE SAUCE..99

CHAPTER SIX: ABOUT THE AUTHOR...................**101**

CHAPTER SEVEN: BONUS CONTENT **104**

CHRISTMAS MARMALADE 104

Chapter One: Introduction to Canning

Historical background

People have been preserving food since the beginning of time. This particular method of preservation originated in France in the 19th century. The French government was looking for a way to make food readily available to the troops year-round so that their military operations were not affected. Nicolas Appert devised a method of canning that laid the stepping stones for what is performed today.

Canning made its advent into America in 1812, when Robert Ayars set up the first canning factory in New York City.

Benefits of canning

By canning, the shelf life of products can be increased significantly, and food remains edible for much longer than it ordinarily would.
Studies have found that canned foods are not lacking in the nutritional value that fresh foods have, and sometimes even serve as healthier alternatives.

Tools needed
- For small-scale canning: A pot that holds enough water to cover the jar you're using
- Foor large-scale canning: A pressure canner and a boiling-water canner
- Jar lifters, to lift hot jars
- Mason jars or Bell jars
- Make sure you have kitchen miscellany like knives, spatulas, and cutting boards at your disposal

Chapter Two: Techniques and Rules

Techniques for preserving food:

Boiling-water method

Boiling-water canners are large kettles made of aluminum or porcelain-covered steel.

This is a lower-temperature process and is more suitable for foods that are highly acidic.

Jars are filled with food and submerged in the boiling water in the canner. The temperature ranges at around 212F. The high level of acidity kills the bacteria and renders the food edible.

Pressure canning method

Pressure canners are essentially heavy pots with tight lids that heat foods to high temperatures.

This is the safest method for preserving low-acid foods.

Jars are filled with food and placed in 2-3 inches of water in the canner. The temperature is usually 240F at a pressure that varies depending on altitude.

It is not recommended to process jars in ovens or dishwashers – they are ineffective as methods of preservation and can even prove to be dangerous.

Low-acid foods: most vegetables, soups, seafood, meat
High-acid foods: most fruits, jams, pickled vegetables, salsa

Caution:
The most important thing to be careful about when preserving food for the long-term is food poisoning. Bacteria present in improperly canned food can bring about a deadly version of food poisoning. The only way to avoid this is by following the right guides and techniques and ensuring that all steps are followed correctly.

What and when to can:
It is vital to ensure that only food of the best quality is being canned. Do not use old or moldy looking meat, fruit, or vegetables; always pick the freshest produce. Additionally, food must be canned while it is still fresh. The less time that it is exposed to air, the better.

Canner pressure:

For pressure canning, the appropriate pressure should be selected based on the altitude where you live. As you go higher up, water boils at lower temperatures so if you use the incorrect pressure, all the bacteria might not be killed.

All the cooking times and pressures mentioned in this book are for altitudes of 1,000 feet or less. If you are at an altitude higher than that, add to the mentioned cooking time and adjust the pressure accordingly.

Use the below chart as indicative and adjust the pressure (for pressure canners) for your altitude and add to the process time (for pressure and boiling-water canners) that is recommended in these recipes.

	0-2,000 ft	2,001-4,000 ft	4,001-6,000 ft	6,001-8,000 ft
Pressure	6 lbs	7 lbs	8 lbs	9 lbs
Time: add	5 minutes	10 minutes	15 minutes	20 minutes

Sterilization:

It is crucial that jars are sterilized before the food is put into them. This sterilization can be done by submerging the jars in the canner (or pot) and boiling for about 10 minutes. No food should be processed in a jar that has not been sterilized. Repeat this activity for the jar lids and rings as well.

Methods of packing:

Raw packing: Jars are filled tightly with fresh, unheated food that has been processed in a pressure canner. Boiling hot water is then poured into the jar, covering the food but leaving a bit of space. This headspace is ½ inch from the top of the jar, and should be strictly followed when using this method.

Hot packing: Food is boiled for a few minutes and then transferred into a jar. This is the preferred method for food processed in a boiling-water canner. The color and flavor of foods packed this way are generally superior to those that have been raw-packed.

Sealing jars:

It is crucial that you check whether the lid of the processed jar is sealed tight. Do this by pressing down on the center – it should not move. If it caves in or pops, that means it has not been sealed properly. Ideally, you will know if your seal is good as soon as you take off the band.

Troubleshooting:

If your jar didn't seal properly after processing or if you're looking at the jars a few months later and the seal appears to have broken, *do not consume*!

Ensure that you detoxify the jars by placing them in a boiling-water canner and boiling for 20 minutes. Cool and dispose of the containers and their contents. Use gloves while performing this package – the spoiled food might contain bacteria which could enter through the skin and prove to be fatal.

If the jar has been sealed properly but you suspect that the food is spoilt, dispose of it immediately.

Storing canned goods:

Store your jars away from direct sunlight in a cool area. Sunlight can spoil the quality of the product, so keep it somewhere that is dark and dry.

How and where you store your jars will determine how long the food will keep without spoiling, so ensure you do this with care.

Handy tip: be sure to label your jars so that you can keep track of how much longer they can be consumed for.

Last words:

Always follow recipes precisely. Tweaking a quantity here or an ingredient there might have unforeseen consequences.

One rule of thumb is to never double recipes – it is always easier to make two smaller batches and have complete control over your recipe than double it and end up with a disaster on your hands.

All these practices ensure that oxygen is removed from the jars and bacteria and mold are killed. If vacuum-packed properly, the jars keep liquid in and air out.

Follow all these rules rigorously and you will produce jars that can be consumed for years together. Happy canning!

Chapter Three: Canning Vegetables

Remember:

- Sterilize your jars before using them.
- Ensure that the jars are hot when you are filling them.
- Always leave headspace while fillings jars – ½ inch at the top.
- Close the jars tightly and seal them with the lid and band before placing in canner.
- After processing, remove band and ensure that the jars have been sealed properly.

Pickles

Time: 13 hours (including wait time)
Makes: 6 pint jars

Ingredients:

- Cucumbers – 8 lbs
- Water – 2 gallons for brining
- Canning/pickling salt – 1 ¼ cups
- Vinegar – 1 ½ quarts
- Sugar – ¼ cup
- Water – 2 quarts for pickle mix
- Mustard seeds – 3 tbsp
- Dill – 14 heads
- Salt – ¾ cup

Method:

Brine:

1. Pick cucumbers that are fresh, dark green, firm, crispy, and not overripe.

2. Dissolve ¾ cup salt in 2 gallons of cold water.

3. Pour this over the cucumbers and let it stand for 12 hours.

4. Discard the liquid.

5. Wash and chop the cucumbers into whatever shape you like.

Pickle mix:

6. Combine the vinegar, sugar and 2 quarts of water along with ½ cup of salt and bring to a boil.

7. Fill the jars with cucumbers, dill, and mustard seeds.

8. Pour hot pickle mix over it and close tightly.

9. Put the jars in the boiling-water canner, and boil for 10 minutes. The longer you boil, the less crisp the cucumbers will be.

Quick Pickles

Time: 5 hours (including wait time)

Makes: 8 pint jars

Ingredients:

- Cucumbers – 6 lbs
- Onions – 3 lbs
- Pickling salt – ½ cup
- Vinegar – 4 cups
- Sugar – 4 ½ cups
- Mustard seeds – 2 tbsp

- Celery seeds – 1 ½ tbsp.
- Ground turmeric – 1 tbsp

Method:

1. Wash and chop cucumbers and onions.

2. Combine cucumbers and onions in a bowl with salt.

3. Cover with ice and refrigerate for 5 hours, adding more ice when necessary.

4. Drain the water out.

5. Combine remaining ingredients in a pot and boil for 10 minutes.

6. Add cucumbers and onions and boil for 3 more minutes.

7. Fill hot jars with the concoction and seal tight.

8. Let it sit undisturbed for 4-5 weeks

Garlic Dill Pickles

Time: 30 minutes

Makes: 4 pint jars

Ingredients:

- Cucumbers – 10
- Vinegar – 2 cups
- Water – 2 cups
- Salt – 2 tbsp
- Dill seeds – 2 tbsp
- Garlic – 6 cloves
- Peppercorns – 2 tsp

Method:

1. Chop the cucumbers.
2. Combine vinegar, water and salt and boil.
3. Separate the garlic, dill seeds and peppercorns equally between the jars.
4. Pack the cucumbers tightly into the jars.
5. Pour the hot liquid into the jars.
6. Process in boiling-water bath for 10 minutes.

Jalapeno Rings

Time: 20 minutes

Makes: 2 pint jars

Ingredients:

- Jalapeno peppers – 10
- Water – ¾ cup
- Vinegar – ¾ cup
- Granulated sugar – 3 tbsp
- Salt – 1 tbsp
- Oregano – 1 tsp

Method:

1. Combine all ingredients except peppers and bring to a rolling boil.
2. Pack jalapeno peppers into jars.
3. Pour hot vinegar mixture onto peppers.
4. Process in boiling-water bath for 10 minutes.

Tomato Salsa

Time: 90 minutes

Makes: 8 pint jars

Ingredients:

- Tomatoes – 12 cups

- Onions – 2 cups

- Cucumbers – 1 cup

- Peppers (green/red/jalapeno) – 3

- Garlic – 2 tbsp

- Sugar – 4 tbsp

- Salt – 2 tsp

- Vinegar – 1 ½ cups

Method:

1. Chop the vegetables.

2. Combine all the ingredients in a pot and boil for 45 minutes. It should reduce by half and thicken.

3. Pour into prepared jars and process in boiling-water canner for 20 minutes.

Onion Jam

Time: 2 hours

Makes: 2 pint jars

Ingredients:

- Onions – 1 lb
- Sugar – 1 cup
- White vinegar – 2 cups
- Water – ¾ cup
- Salt – 2 tbsp

Method:

1. Chop the onions.

2. Combine sugar, water, vinegar on a low flame until the sugar dissolves.

3. Add the onions.

4. Bring to a boil and cook for 1 hour or until the onions are translucent.

5. Remove from heat and refrigerate once cool.

Corn Relish

Time: 20 minutes

Makes: 2 pint jars

Ingredients:

- Corn, cooked – 2 cups
- Peppers – ½ cup
- Onion – 1
- Garlic – 2 cloves
- Vinegar – 2/3 cup
- Sugar – 2 tbsp

- Salt – 2 tbsp
- Spices of your choice

Method:

1. Combine corn with chopped vegetables, vinegar, sugar, and salt.

2. Bring to a boil and then simmer for 7 minutes.

3. Cool and refrigerate.

Carrot and Cabbage Jars

Time: 40 minutes

Makes: 5 pint jars

Ingredients:

- Carrots – 2 lbs

- Cabbage – 2 lbs

- Water

- Salt

Method:

1. Wash, peel and grate the carrots and cabbage.

2. Pack them tightly into jars.

3. Pour boiling water over the carrots leaving headspace.

4. Add salt.

5. Process in pressure canner for 20 minutes at 10 lbs pressure.

Cauliflower Zucchini Preserve

Time: 2.5 hours (including wait time)

Makes: 4 pint jars

Ingredients:

- Cauliflowers – 2 heads
- Zucchini – 1 cup
- Onions – 3
- Mustard seeds – 1 tbsp
- Turmeric – 1 tsp

- Vinegar – 4 cups
- Sugar – 2 cups
- Salt

Method:

1. Wash and cut cauliflowers, zucchini, and onions.

2. Combine with salt and cover with ice.

3. Let it stand for two hours in the refrigerator, adding ice when necessary.

4. Combine remaining ingredients and bring to a boil.

5. Pack vegetables in jars and pour hot liquid into it.

6. Process in boiling-water canner for 10 minutes.

Pepper Garlic Jelly

Time: 30 minutes

Makes: 3 pint jars

Ingredients:

- Peppers – 2 cups
- Jalapenos – ½ cup
- Garlic – 10 cloves
- Vinegar – 2 cups
- Sugar – 4 cups
- Pectin – 3 tsp

Method:

1. Combine peppers, garlic and vinegar and bring to a boil.

2. Add sugar and pectin and boil until sugar dissolves.

3. Fill jars with the mixture.

4. Process in boiling-water bath for 15 minutes.

Sweet Potatoes

Time: 90 minutes

Makes: 10 pint jars

Ingredients:

- Sweet potatoes – 2 lbs

- Sugar

- Water

Method:

1. Peel and chop sweet potatoes.

2. Combine sugar and water and bring to a boil until mixture thickens.

3. Pack sweet potatoes into jars and ladle hot liquid into it.

4. Process in pressure canner for 1 hour at 10 lbs pressure.

Pickled Beets

Time: 45 minutes

Makes: 6 pint jars

Ingredients:

- Beets – 6

- Sugar – 2 cups

- Vinegar – 1 ½ cups

- Water – 2 ½ cups

- Salt – 1 tbsp

- Cloves – ¼ cup

Method:

1. Cover chopped beets in water and cook for 30 minutes, until soft.

2. Combine sugar, water, cloves, and vinegar and boil for 10 minutes.

3. Fill the beets into jars and pour boiling water on top.

4. Process in boiling-water canner for 10 minutes.

Canned Asparagus

Time: 30 minutes

Makes: 3 pint jars

Ingredients:

- Asparagus – 20

- Salt – 2 tbsp

- Water – 5 cups

- Chili flakes – 1 tbsp

- Sugar – ¼ cup

Method:

1. Chop asparagus finely and boil for 5 minutes.

2. Combine sugar, vinegar, salt, and water.

3. Boil until sugar dissolves.

4. Pack tightly into jars.

5. Pour sugar mixture into jars.

6. Process in boiling-water canner for 10 minutes.

Pumpkin Butter

Time: 30 minutes

Makes: 3 pint jars

Ingredients:

- Pumpkin puree – 30 oz (canned or fresh)
- Granulated sugar – ½ cup
- Brown sugar – ½ cup
- 100% pure apple juice or apple cider – 1 cup
- Ground cinnamon – 2 tsp
- Ground ginger – 1 tsp
- Freshly grated whole nutmeg – ¾ tsp
- Ground cloves – ½ tsp
- Lemon juice – 2 tsp

Method:

1. Combine all ingredients and cook on medium-high for 20-25 minutes until thick and spreadable.
2. Transfer to airtight container and refrigerate once cool.

Lime Jelly

Time: 40 minutes

Makes: 4 pint jars

Ingredients:

- Limes – 10
- Water – 2 cups
- Sugar – 4 cups
- Pectin – 3 oz

Method:

1. Grate the peel of the limes and squeeze the juice out of them.

2. Combine lime juice, peel, water, and sugar in a pan.

3. Bring to a rolling boil, stirring constantly.

4. And pectin and boil for 2 more minutes.

5. Ladle into jars and process in boiling-water canner for 10 minutes.

Green Beans

Time: 30 minutes

Makes: 4 pint jars

Ingredients:

- Beans – 2 lbs

- Water

Method:

1. Wash the beans and chop off the stems.

2. Chop into whatever size you like.

3. Pack tightly into jars, and pour boiling water into the jar.

4. Process in pressure canner for 20 minutes at 10 lbs pressure.

5. Allow to cool for a few hours.

Rhubarb

Time: 30 minutes

Makes: 2 pint jars

Ingredients:

- Sliced rhubarb – 1 ½ cups

- Sugar – 1 ½ cups

Method:

1. Combine rhubarb and sugar until the juices start flowing.

2. Bring to a gentle boil and stir constantly.

3. Ladle into prepared jars and process in boiling water canner for 15 minutes.

Mixed Vegetable Jar

Time: 30 minutes

Makes: 4 pint jars

Ingredients:

- Cucumbers – 3
- Carrots – 4
- Zucchini – 1
- Peppers – 2
- Squash – 1
- Sugar – 3 tsp
- Salt – 3 tbsp
- Vinegar – 1 cup
- Water – 2 cups

Method:

1. Chop all the vegetables and boil for 5 minutes.

2. Combine sugar, water, salt, vinegar, and water.

3. Bring to a boil.

4. Pack vegetables tightly into jars.

5. Pour hot liquid into jars.

6. Process in boiling-water canner for 10 minutes.

Chapter Four: Fruit Canning

Strawberry Jam

Time: 45 minutes

Makes: 4 pint jars

Ingredients:

- Hulled and mashed strawberries – 3 lbs
- Lemon juice – ¼ cup
- Powdered pectin – 6 tbsp
- Granulated sugar – 7 cups
- Butter – 1 tbsp

Method:

1. Combine strawberries, butter and lemon juice in a saucepan.
2. Add pectin and bring it to a rolling boil. Do not stop stirring!
3. Add sugar and let it dissolve into the mixture. Boil for 1 minute.
4. Remove from heat.
5. Transfer hot jam into hot jars and process in boiling-water canner for 10 minutes.
6. Allow it to sit undisturbed for 36 hours.

Quick Strawberry Jam

Time: 60 minutes

Makes: 4 pint jars

Ingredients:

- Hulled and mashed strawberries – 3 lbs
- Lemon juice – ¼ cup
- Powdered pectin – 6 tbsp
- Granulated sugar – 7 cups
- Butter – 1 tbsp

Method:

1. Let all the ingredients except the lemon juice stew on a low flame for 45 minutes.

2. Add lemon juice and bring to a boil for 10 minutes. Do not allow it to scorch. Keep stirring.

3. Pour into hot jars and allow to cool on countertop for 6-8 hours.

4. Refrigerate once cool.

Blueberry Jam

Time: 40 minutes

Makes: 1 pint jar

Ingredients:

- Blueberries – 3 cups
- Sugar – ¼ cup
- Lemon juice – 2 tsp

Method:

1. Combine all the ingredients with a pinch of salt in a saucepan.
2. Mash until the juice oozes out of the fruit.
3. Cook for 20 minutes, until it thickens.
4. Refrigerate once cool.

Fig Jam

Time: 90 minutes

Makes: 2 pint jars

Ingredients:

- Figs – 2 lbs

- Sugar – 1 ½ cups

- Lemon juice – ¼ cup

Method:

1. Combine all ingredients and simmer for 60-75 minutes, stirring continuously until it thickens.

2. Fill jars with the mixture.

3. Process in boiling-water canner for 10 minutes.

Apple Banana Butter

Time: 2 ½ hours

Makes: 3 pint jars

Ingredients:

- Apples – 2 lbs

- Bananas – 3

- Sugar – ¾ cup

- Water – 1 cup

Method:

1. Combine all ingredients and cook for 2 hours.

2. Fill into jars.

3. Process in boiling-water canner for 7 minutes.

Apricot Jam

Time: 40 minutes

Makes: 3 pint jars

Ingredients:

- Apricots, chopped – 4 cups

- Lemon juice – 5 tbsp

- Sugar – 3 cups

Method:

1. Combine all ingredients and bring to a boil.

2. Simmer for 20 minutes, until it thickens.

3. Fill jars with the mixture.

4. Process in boiling-water bath for 10 minutes.

Peach Preserve

Time: 45 minutes

Makes: 3 pint jars

Ingredients:

- Peaches – 15

- Sugar – 4 cups

- Pectin – 2 oz

Method:

1. Add chopped peaches and bring to a boil over medium-low heat for 15 minutes until peaches soften.

2. Add sugar and boil once again until the mixture thickens.

3. Transfer into prepared jars and process in boiling-water canner for 10 minutes.

Apple Butter

Time: 45 minutes

Makes: 3 pint jars

Ingredients:

- Apples – 14

- Water – 2 cups

- Sugar – 3 cups

- Cinnamon – 3 tsp

Method:

1. Core, peel and cut apples.

2. Combine apples with water and cook until soft. Puree.

3. Add sugar and cinnamon.

4. Boil over medium heat until it thickens.

5. Ladle into prepared jars and process in boiling-water canner for 10 minutes.

Pina Colada Jelly

Time: 25 minutes

Makes: 2 pints

Ingredients:

- Pineapple, chopped – 1

- Coconut cream – 1/3 cup

- Pectin – 3 oz

- Butter – ¼ tsp

- Sugar – 3 cups

- Coconut – ½ cup

Method:

1. Crush the pineapple and add it to a pot with pectin.

2. Pour coconut cream, sugar, and butter over it.

3. Boil for 10 minutes.

4. Pour into sterilized jars and process in boiling-water canner for 5 minutes.

Optional: you can use coconut rum or coconut water instead of coconut cream. Do not use coconut milk.

Honeyed Oranges

Time: 70 minutes

Makes: 2 pint jars

Ingredients:

- Oranges – 3 lbs

- Sugar – 1 ½ cups

- Honey – 1 ½ cups

- Lemon juice – 5 tsp

- Spices (cinnamon, cloves, nutmeg)

Method:

1. Chop the oranges and combine, peel included, with water.

2. Bring to a boil and simmer for 20 minutes.

3. Combine remaining ingredients in a separate pan.

4. Bring to a boil, stirring until sugar is dissolved.

5. Add oranges and boil for 45 minutes.

6. Pour into boiling-water canner and process for 15 minutes.

Plums

Time: 30 minutes

Makes: 3 pint jars

Ingredients:

- Plums – 2 lbs

- Water – 2 ½ cups

- Honey – 1 cup

- Orange juice – ½ cup

- Cinnamon powder – 1 tsp

Method:

1. Combine water, honey, and orange juice.

2. Bring to a boil and simmer for 5 minutes.

3. Add chopped plums and cinnamon powder to the mixture.

4. Boil until plums soften.

5. Fill the jars with the mixture.

6. Process in a boiling-water canner for 15 minutes.

Spiced Cherries and Raspberries

Time: 60 minutes

Makes: 3 pint jars

Ingredients:

- Cherries – 1 lb

- Raspberries – 1 lb

- Water – 3 cups

- Sugar – 1 cup

- Vinegar – 1 ½ cups

- Cinnamon powder – 2 tbsp

- Cloves – 4

Method:

1. Combine water, sugar, and spices and boil until sugar dissolves.

2. Add the cherries and raspberries and simmer for 15 minutes.

3. Add the honey and vinegar and boil for 15 more minutes.

4. Transfer the figs into jars and pour the hot liquid over it.

5. Process in boiling-water canner for 15 minutes.

Banana Butter

Time: 30 minutes

Makes: 3 pint jars

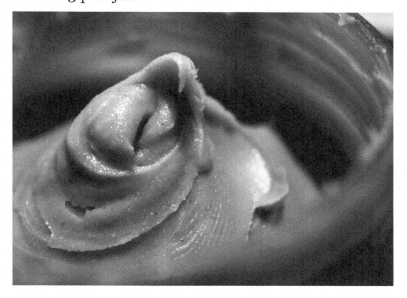

Ingredients:

- Bananas – 5
- Chopped pineapple – 3 cups
- Desiccated coconut – ¼ cup
- Sugar – 3 cups
- Lemon juice – 5 tsp
- Water – ¼ cup

Method:

1. Combine all ingredients in a pot and bring to a boil.

2. Cook until the mixture thickens.

3. Transfer into jars.

4. Process in boiling-water bath for 15 minutes.

Chapter Five: More Canning

Yogurt and Berry Parfait

Time: 15 minutes

Makes: 1 pint jar

Ingredients:

- Greek yogurt – 6 oz

- Oats – ½ cup

- Chia seeds – 1 tbsp

- Sunflower seeds – 1 tbsp

- Milk – 4 tbsp

- Berries – 1 cup

Method:

1. Combine yogurt, oats, chia seeds, and milk.

2. Layer half of the mixture at the bottom of a jar.

3. Add fruits on top and then another layer of the remaining yogurt mixture.

Alternatives: quinoa, peaches, nuts, granola, dark chocolate

Jar Cupcakes

Time: 15 minutes

Makes: 4 pint jars

Ingredients:

- Ready-made cupcakes – 8

- Cream cheese frosting – 4 oz

Method:

1. Slice cupcakes horizontally.

2. Place at the bottom of jar.

3. Pipe cream cheese frosting onto the cupcake.

4. Alternate between layers of cake and cream cheese, ending with cake on top.

5. Refrigerate.

Optional: add layers of jelly, custard, or fruit.

Moroccan Salad

Time: 20 minutes

Makes: 1 pint jar

Ingredients:

- Couscous, cooked – 1 cup

- Yogurt – 3 tbsp

- Cucumber, chopped – 1

- Beetroot, grated – ½ lbs

- Oranges, segmented – 3

- Lemon juice – 3 tbsp

- Garlic, chopped – 2 cloves

- Chickpeas – 1 lb

- Olive oil – 1/3 cup

Method:

1. Combine lemon juice, olive oil, garlic, and yogurt.

2. Layer the mixture at the bottom of a jar.

3. Top off with remaining ingredients.

Thai Dipping Sauce

Time: 40 minutes

Makes: 4 pint jars

Ingredients:

- Garlic, minced – 1/3 cup

- Vinegar – 4 cups

- Sugar – 4 cups

- Red pepper flakes – ½ cup

- Salt – 1 tbsp

Method:

1. Heat vinegar. Add sugar to it and boil until it dissolves.

2. Add garlic, pepper flakes, salt.

3. Boil for 2 minutes.

4. Ladle into prepared jars and process in boiling-water canner for 15 minutes.

Caramel Corn With Nuts

Time: 90 minutes

Makes: One standard size tray

Ingredients:

- Popped popcorn – 10 cups

- Brown sugar – 1 cup

- Butter – ½ cup

- Corn syrup – ¼ cup

- Salt – ¼ tsp

- Baking soda – ¼ tsp

- Mixed nuts – 1 cup

Method:

1. Spread popcorn on a baking tray.

2. Combine brown sugar, butter, corn syrup, and salt in a saucepan and cook for 15-20 minutes, until small amounts of mixture dropped in cold water forms a ball.

3. Add soda.

4. Pour the above mixture over popcorn.

5. Sprinkle nuts.

6. Bake at 220F for 40 minutes.

7. Cool and break into pieces. Store in jars.

Barbecue Sauce

Time: 60 minutes

Makes: 4 pint jars

Ingredients:

- Onions – 3

- Garlic – 5 cloves

- Oil – 1 tbsp

- Tomato sauce – 6 cups

- Vinegar – 1 ½ cups

- Chili powder – 4 tbsp

- Paprika – 2 tsp

- Honey – ½ cup

- Salt

Method:

1. Saute the onions and garlic in oil.

2. Add all the other ingredients and bring to a boil.

3. Simmer for 45 minutes.

4. Transfer into jars.

5. Process in boiling-water canner for 20 minutes.

Chapter Six: About the Author

Paul Batali, born 1975 in Marseille, France. In 1993, at age 18 he immigrated to the United States and at the age of 22, traveled to France to study Biochemistry. During his studies, he decided that he wanted to learn cooking after seeing a random hotel school ad on the Metro. He went on to graduate from the school with high grades in 2002.

Batali lived in France until 2003, working in local restaurants and with international chefs. He then returned to the United States where he worked for a year as a department chef at the Wellington Hotel. He later served as the first chef of the Bambo Dlug restaurant in Alabama, and for three years was the first chef of Dan Kramer's Delidog. He also served as the first chef at the 122 Fish Restaurant at the State Junction for two years.

In December 2008, together with Jack Dolan, he opened the Chloelys Restaurant, located on the Mississippi Exchange complex, named after his two daughters, Jennifer and Emily. The restaurant specializes in fish and seafood, and among its raw materials are langoustines, dolphinfish, and Italian duck. The restaurant has both meat and vegetarian options. The kitchen is open and allows diners to watch the dishes being prepared. In the front of the kitchen is an aquarium with lobsters and a display window displaying the fish imported from the ends of the earth,

The restaurant won a prize for excellence in the years 2010-2011 from the Shine Spectator Magazine for its canning preparation containing 6,000 jars of 120 varieties.

Chapter Seven: Bonus Content

Christmas Marmalade

Time: 100 minutes

Makes: 4 pint jars

Ingredients:

- Oranges, grapefruit, lemons – 2 lbs

- Cinnamon powder – 2 tsp

- Cloves – ½ tsp

- Cardamom pods – 4

- Water – 4 cups

- Sugar – 1 lbs

Method:

1. Juice, zest and chop up the fruit.

2. Add the fruit, juices, spices, and water and bring to a boil.

3. Simmer for 45 minutes.

4. Add sugar and boil until the mixture reaches 223F, about 20 minutes.

5. Ladle the mixture into jars.

6. Process in a boiling-water canner for 10 minutes.